GIVERNY
The garden of Claude Monet

Photography by Brigitte and Philippe Perdereau

INTRODUCTION

Gilbert Vahé

Head gardener since the recreation of the garden in 1976

It was meant to be an easy, routine job: when I first started work at Giverny, in October 1976, the abandoned, long-forgotten garden was to be brought back to life to welcome around 7,000 visitors a year. The care of Claude Monet's garden had been gradually neglected by his descendants; four years of work were needed to totally reconstruct the garden before it could be opened to the public. But who, apart from "the painter who loved flowers", could sensitively take charge of this horticultural masterpiece from the early 20th century?

Another artist, himself a painter – and who, strangely enough, had some friends who had visited Monet in their youth – felt the same passion for Giverny that Monet had done. He, too, had discovered that very special light that, on certain mornings at dawn, bathes the whole countryside in rosy pink. After managing the restoration of Versailles, Gerald Van der Kemp came to settle at Giverny, and he offered me the chance to recreate, in its entirety, the garden that had been such an inspiration to Monet, to give back to the *Clos Normand* and the Water Garden all the special qualities that they had in his time. Madame Van der Kemp's fund-raising skills and good business sense allowed enough money to be raised in just a few months to restore Giverny and open it to the public. It was an unbelievable success. In that first year, 70,000 visitors crowded the garden's paths: a disaster for the garden, which was never meant to have so many visitors!

Today the numbers are even greater: 400,000 to 500,000 come each year to admire the fruits of our labours. Ten gardeners are constantly at work, striving to keep the garden fresh and looking as

much as possible like the one that Monet knew, as well as to make sure that it provides an unbroken succession of flowers from its opening day in April until it closes at the end of October.

Each one of the gardeners is, in a small way, a guardian of Monet's spirit. If we adapt the plantings, introducing cultivars or even species that were not widely available, if at all, in the artist's time, it is always with respect for the colours, harmonies and general appearance that the visitors like to rediscover, season after season and year after year. On the other hand, our work is not limited by strict plans or absolute rules, and our individual experience as gardeners allows each of us to decide where and how to set out the plants to give the best effect.

We produce most of the plants on site, so as to be able to place them and plant them at the ideal moment, but also to be sure of growing our chosen cultivars and getting the precise colours that we want. Cuttings are taken, seeds sown and any heavy work is undertaken in the second half of autumn and during winter, so that any changes made at other times can be done as discreetly as possible. In early summer, however, alert visitors may notice, round the corner of a flowerbed, one of us lifting a faded spring-bedding plant to replace it with one for summer. The spectacle must never cease.

Giverny allows you not only to enter the living pictures that inspired the painter, but also to take a leap back into history. It is a fabulous testimony to how a garden was conceived and planted a hundred years ago, at the time when French horticulture was still at its peak. This kind of intensive planting, based on bulbs, annuals and perennials, is at once very horticultural and structured, yet also very natural, because the design of the borders is modelled on the way that plants grow together in the wild. The influence of nature is even more obvious in the Water Garden, where there are more trees, shrubs and bamboos.

It is, moreover, nature itself that dictates the calendar of flowering-times: never exactly the same, it forces the gardeners to know how to adapt to its conditions to bring forward or delay such operations as pricking out and transplanting. No-one, therefore, can guarantee the flowering time of irises, poppies, wisteria or roses to within a week or so, but we do everything that we can to make them last as long as possible, by choosing cultivars that do not all flower at the same time. However, we will never be able to control the flowering of the waterlilies, as they need a minimum temperature of 16°C for a month before coming into flower.

So, as it turns out, working at Giverny has never been easy, let alone routine. Year follows year with no two ever the same and, like all gardeners, we are always planning for the future, constantly preparing for next spring. No doubt it will seem much the same as all the springs that have gone before it, except for one or two details that will stand out as being interesting differences. Above all, because of Giverny's position at the confluence of the valleys of the Epte and the Seine, there will be this particularly magical light; the same light that Monet found here, and that even the flowers seem to love.

THE *CLOS NORMAND* (p.26)

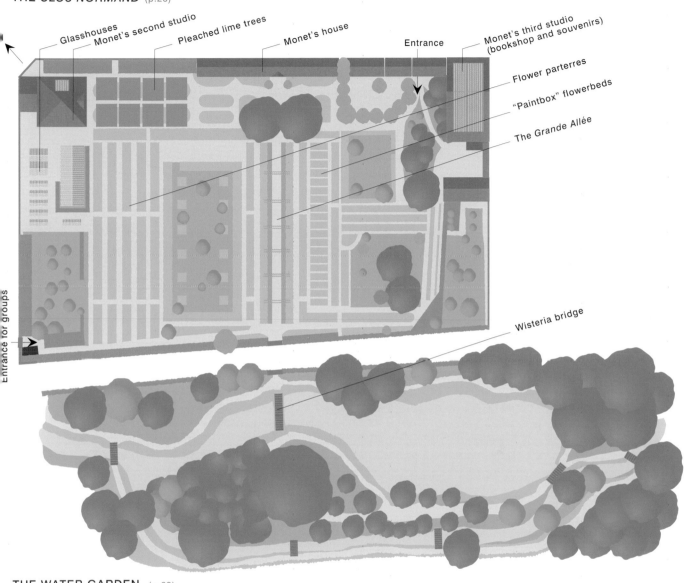

Glasshouses
Monet's second studio
Pleached lime trees
Monet's house
Entrance
Monet's third studio (bookshop and souvenirs)
Flower parterres
"Paintbox" flowerbeds
The Grande Allée
Wisteria bridge

Entrance for groups

THE WATER GARDEN (p.68)

DOUBLE-PAGE OVERLEAF:
Two views, looking towards Monet's second studio.

In June (LEFT-HAND PAGE), an abundance of dame's violet (*Hesperis matronalis*) in mauve and white fills the border. Also commonly known as sweet rocket, these biennial plants are set out in autumn. They flower alongside climbing roses trained on vertical tripods; their flowers echo the bushes of *Rosa* 'Santa Catalina' trained against the walls, just below the windows.

In October (RIGHT-HAND PAGE), perennial sunflowers (*Helianthus decapetalus*) take their turn to fill the borders, giving them a lovely, luminous golden glow that contrasts well with the blue of the asters. These are also perennials and rapidly take over the flowerbeds. In November, the gardeners will uproot some of them to make way for new plantings.

→ THE GARDEN PICTURE
THE ART OF TRANSFORMATION

Claude Monet's gardens provide an unbroken
succession of flowers from April right through
until November. The gardeners arrange
for several "waves" of flowering by making
use of different kinds of plant:
bulbs, biennials, annuals, perennials,
trees and shrubs, not forgetting climbers.
Constant maintenance and the replacement
of fading and underperforming plants ensure
the continuing existence of a perfect picture
– indeed, many such perfect pictures.
Each flowerbed is designed as a tapestry in
four dimensions: on the ground, vertically,
and through time, so that all of their varied
elements follow on from each other without
interrupting the magical interplay of colours.

RIGHT
At the beginning of spring (April), this
flowerbed is a tapestry of wallflowers
and Spanish bluebells (*Hyacinthoides
hispanica*). In the background a large
Clematis montana festoons
the metal framework.

In spring, the raised terrace by the house is adorned with Chinese pots planted
with young flowering crab apples (*Malus floribunda*) surrounded by cinerarias
(*Pericallis* x *hybrida*). The roses on the trellis have scarcely reawoken,
but orange crown imperials (*Fritillaria imperialis*) dominate the flowerbeds.

In summer, the Chinese pots are embellished with marguerites
(*Argyranthemum frutescens*, syn. *Chrysanthemum frutescens*) trained
as standards. Amongst the different roses, 'Aimée Vibert' (white) and
'American Pillar' (pink) harmonise with the colour of the facade.

Late May, and the border edgings of purple aubrietia (*Aubrieta deltoidea*)
come into flower at the same time as the tall bearded iris cultivars,
but their mauve colouring will last for several more weeks
to accompany the mauve or white dame's violet (*Hesperis matronalis*).

By late summer, the vegetation has grown much taller, with red, white and
pink cosmos (*Cosmos bipinnatus*), white or bluish asters (*Aster novii-belgii*),
and the tall perennial sunflowers (*Helianthus decapetalus*), whose foliage has
taken over from the dame's violet. The irises, divided during summer,
and the trimmed-back aubrietia make an effective, discreet green edging.

At midsummer, the *Grande Allée*, the broad path leading from the house to the front gate, is starting to be overrun by nasturtiums, planted as an edging. They are accompanied by purple loosestrife (*Lythrum salicaria*), gladioli and tobacco plants (*Nicotiana*) in soft pink, garnet-red or white (see details, p.54). On the arches, roses continue to bloom over the course of the weeks.

In October, the abundant flowering reaches its peak in both borders.
Cosmos, nicotiana, asters and perennial sunflowers contrast or harmonise,
each in their own way, with the orange flowers of the nasturtiums, which
now cover almost the full width of the path. The gardeners keep just a
narrow pathway clear to indicate the presence of the *Grande Allée*.

The large rose Centenaire de Lourdes ('Delge'), grown as a standard, is not from Monet's time, but it combines vigour and generosity of bloom with a rather "old-fashioned" character. The weight of its innumerable flesh-pink flowers bows down its supple shoots throughout summer, as it is especially remontant (repeat- or continuous-flowering). Its long flowering season begins in mid-June, when the dame's violets are at their peak.

As they fade, the dame's violets are replaced by cosmos (raised in the nursery and transplanted here at the end of June). They grow rapidly and start flowering around mid-July, not stopping until the frosts. The subtle tones and silky texture of their petals are especially enhanced by the soft, gentle light and early morning dews of September and early October.

Beside the lake, in late April and early May, the fresh colours of the soft green Japanese maple (*Acer palmatum* var. *dissectum*) in the foreground and its red-leaved relative in the background (*A. palmatum* 'Atropurpureum') are just as vivid as the massed flowers of the red Japanese azaleas.

By the end of October, the maple leaves attract attention once again,
turning rust, orange or yellow. The azalea, still green, continues to be
a good contrast, but before long some of its foliage will also colour brightly
(the rest will stay green and hang on for part of the winter).

In May, the famous Japanese bridge that crosses the edge of the
waterlily pond is covered with mauve Chinese wisteria (*Wisteria sinensis*)
before the white-flowered Japanese wisteria (*W. floribunda* 'Alba')
takes over for the end of May and early June.

In autumn, the wisteria foliage turns yellow just before falling, lending a
new magic to the view of the Japanese bridge before winter sets in for good.
Little by little, the tortuous form of the creepers is unveiled against the
unique colour of the handrails.

DOUBLE-PAGE OVERLEAF
Late autumn on the Japanese bridge, with
the last leaves of the weeping willows
lingering on for a few days after the
wisteria has been denuded.

→ THE *CLOS NORMAND*
THROUGH THE SEASONS

The *Clos* is the main part of the Garden of Giverny, the part that includes Monet's house with its distinctive pink walls.

It has a rather strict underlying geometry of mostly long, narrow or rectangular flowerbeds, defined by brick edgings. But this somewhat restrictive layout is greatly softened by the profusion of plants which, from certain viewpoints, allows you to forget the pathways and the pattern of the garden. The flowers, all planted in generous quantities, bloom in turn over the course of the seasons so that the borders are always colourful and never give the slightest impression of emptiness.

A mixture of rigour and generosity, structure and abundance, this typically French garden is just as attractive as a whole as it is in the fine detail of its plant associations, which are easy to copy and adapt.

RIGHT
Beneath the arch covered with *Rosa* 'Albertine', the dame's violets (*Hesperis matronalis*) are spangled with the spherical flowerheads of *Allium hollandicum*.

As in Monet's day, by careful selection of cultivars it is possible to achieve
a long flowering season. When the first daffodils fade (foreground),
later-flowering cultivars (such as the white ones just behind the tree)
follow on to make a link to the first tulips.

LEFT
The opening of the garden, in April, is marked by masses of flowering
bulbs, with yellow or white narcissus and blue hyacinths being the first
to appear. In the orchard, these flowers are planted
in large squares in the grass.

Small or medium-sized pansies and violas have spreading growth that makes a good carpet for the soil between taller plants. They hide the fading foliage of small bulbs as it dies back, and harmonise well with the bluish leaves of poppies and nasturtiums (lower right).

A detail of a mixture of red, white and blue pansies accompanied by
pink and blue hyacinths. The large leaves belong to tulips that
will flower soon afterwards (the buds are visible on the
ones at the top of the picture).

A carpet of wallflowers (*Erysimum cheiri*, syn. *Cheiranthus cheiri*),
with golden and pale yellow flowers, lights up the feet of the flowering
crab apples planted in front of the house. Wallflowers are often used as a foil
for bulbs, but they are also magnificent when grouped together, especially
when the colour associations are close ones, not a bright and garish mix.

RIGHT

Mimosa-yellow tulip 'Olympic Flame' is
irregularly flamed with red; the two tints
are repeated in the carpet of pansies
and wallflowers beneath them.

Even though this association of pink tulips (Triumph Group cultivars, opening in April and early May) and forget-me-nots has become very traditional, it is nevertheless spectacular. The young forget-me-not plants are set out in November, just after (and just on top of) the tulip bulbs. All the bedding is dug up around mid-May to make way for a planting of red or pink pelargoniums that will, in their turn, make a brightly coloured carpet beneath the rose stems.

The apple trees in the orchard echo the colours of the house, whereas the
yellow daffodils and the first tulips are a livelier counterpoint to this rather
gentle harmony. Although Monet was fond of monochrome colour schemes,
he did not mind catching the eye with a few splashes of contrasting tones.

In this other corner of the orchard, harmony reigns between the white
blossom of the apple trees and the gentle tints of the pale yellow narcissi.
In the distance you catch a glimpse of the pink tulips growing in the border
just in front of the house.

The flowering crab apples scattered through the flowerbeds accompany and enrich the display of the apples grown for fruit in the orchard. Here, a superb weeping cultivar (*Malus* x *gloriosa* 'Oekonomierat Echtermeyer', often simply known as 'Echtermeyer') marks the end of a long border.

This Japanese ornamental crab apple (*Malus floribunda*) is surrounded by a carpet of pale yellow wallflower, *Erysimum* 'Moonlight' (syn. *Cheiranthus* 'Moonlight'). Because the tree flowers so heavily, its rate of growth is quite slow, which is a distinct advantage in a flowerbed.

This white clematis montana (*Clematis montana* var. *grandiflora*) trained along horizontal metal supports, frames the floral tableau, here consisting mainly of mauve dame's violet (also known as sweet rocket) with, in the foreground, a few late tulips of a similar hue.

Allium hollandicum 'Purple Sensation' produces beautiful mauve spheres in perfect harmony with the dame's violet that is in full flower at the same time. This kind of detail, gradually revealed as you walk between the plants along the garden paths, adds greatly to the enjoyment of a visit.

Dutch irises (*Iris x hollandica*) are planted as bulbs in autumn or very early spring. They flower slightly later than the bearded irises (mid- to late June) and come back reliably year after year. This beautiful white and yellow cultivar is sailing through a foaming sea of lady's mantle (*Alchemilla mollis*).

DOUBLE-PAGE SPREAD, PAGES 44–45
Seen crossways on, looking towards the house at an angle, the paths disappear, transforming the garden into a vast field of flowers with the same colours echoing back and forth. Blue, mauve and white irises harmonise with white or mauve dame's violet until the first roses appear.

Various peonies punctuate the flowerbeds. Some of the older cultivars were contemporaries of the painter. He would, no doubt, have loved this one, *Paeonia lactiflora* 'Nippon Brilliant', a "Japanese" (or "anemone centred") cultivar raised in 1933 in the United States, with rich but subtle colours that harmonise for several days with those of the oriental poppies. Around the peony wave the stems of perennial *Anthemis tinctoria*; its yellow daisies will open once the peonies and poppies have faded.

A superb harmony, between the dame's violet and the upright clusters of flowers on the large *Paulownia* in the background. This echo of colours makes a perfect link between the two parts of the garden, the *Clos Normand* and the Water Garden. Later (page 69) we will see how it does so.

RIGHT
Monet also loved flowering shrubs, which were then becoming popular. Close by the gardener's house, two beautiful rhododendron bushes take their turn to adorn themselves in the mauve that dominates the garden at this season.

The arches that crown the "paintbox" beds are clad in roses and other climbers, such as this large-flowered clematis ('Doctor Ruppel'). This clematis flowers for the first time in May and June, then reprises its performance at the end of summer, at which time it harmonises equally well with the mauve and blue tints of the asters.

A superb modern climbing rose ('Santa Catalina') clothes the wooden panelling and exposed beams of Monet's second studio. This cultivar was an obvious choice because of its long flowering period, all through summer, whereas the roses from Monet's time only bloom in June and July.

The gardeners also introduced modern shrub roses, more disease-resistant and above all more "remontant" (flowering continuously throughout summer) than older cultivars. Priority was, however, given to ones with an "old-fashioned" appearance, such as this English Rose, Mary Rose ('Ausmary').

White rose 'Aimée Vibert' flowers over a long period in summer. In July it is joined by 'American Pillar', an old climbing rose cultivar, but still very popular for its clear, bright pink colour. On the right is a beautiful white rose, grown as a standard: Iceberg ('Korbin', syn. *Fée des Neiges*). At this time of year, the Chinese pots are planted with clipped cones of bay (*Laurus nobilis*).

If trained carefully as a standard, a rose can be turned into a small tree.
It must, nevertheless, still be pruned (as discreetly as possible), especially
when its crown begins to fill out, gaining volume and therefore weight.
After echoing the pink of the tamarisk (on the left, in the foreground), this
pink rose now offsets the mauve dame's violets, the whole scheme being
carefully enlivened by white oxeye daisies (*Leucanthemum vulgare*).

RIGHT
Because space is so limited in the
flowerbeds, Monet used several different
ingenious ways to raise up his roses so as
to be able to plant other flowers beneath
them. Thus we find numerous roses
grown on single stems as standards or
half-standards, but also quite a few
climbing or shrub roses trained onto
the metal arches or columns
(all painted the same shade of green)
that is so typical of Giverny.

Flowering tobacco (*Nicotiana affinis*) in white (and innumerable other colours too) flowers all along the *Grande Allée* the whole summer through. Some colours are more perfumed than others and their scent is most noticeable in the late afternoon.

The bizarre flowers of *Cleome spinosa* resemble large insects. In flower over a long period, from July to October, they continue to produce new blooms as the stems lengthen. Single-flowered *Cosmos bipinnatus* makes a perfect companion for them.

In 2008, the floral décor of the *Grande Allée* was dominated by purple loosestrife (*Lythrum salicaria*), mixed with mauve zinnias, red or white nicotiana, and, of course, nasturtiums (the round leaves in the foreground).

At the shady end of one flowerbed, two unusual hardy plants: a pink begonia (*Begonia grandis* subsp. *evansiana*) and an impatiens (*Impatiens balfourii*). Although most of their relatives cannot stand the frost, these two return faithfully each year because their seeds and corms are able to withstand the cold of our winters. They flower abundantly, from mid-August right up to the first frosts.

RIGHT
The flowering of meadow saffron (*Colchicum autumnale*) in the orchard lawns announces the end of summer. These "naked ladies" arise from large underground bulbs which do not produce their leaves until the following spring.

Close-up of a nasturtium (*Tropaeolum majus*) in flower, showing the distinctive, almost circular, shape of its leaves.

Annual rudbeckia flowers (*Rudbeckia hirta*), alongside a purple amaranth (*Amaranthus paniculatus*).

LEFT

In September, the *Grande Allée* is impassable, completely overrun by a carpet of nasturtiums, normally climbing plants but here persuaded to scramble across the gravel. The gardeners take care to mix the different colours – orange, yellow and red – in order to avoid monotony and to delight the onlooker's eye as it follows the narrow pathway that is deliberately kept clear between the two banks of this river of nasturtiums.

A giant-flowered dahlia, planted close to the edge of the paths so that its immense flowerheads can be easily admired.

White flowers help to calm down a colour scheme, even white cactus dahlias (here accompanied by blue and white asters).

LEFT

The *Clos Normand* owes a large part of its summer show to dahlias; many and varied, they enliven the flowerbeds from August until the frosts. Monet loved the tallest, most opulent cultivars with their spectacular blooms. Their sometimes rather heavy appearance can be softened by surrounding them with the much daintier flowers of cosmos (*C. bipinnatus*).

In the first years after the restoration of the garden, the dahlias helped to bring a feeling of maturity to the flowerbeds, not only by their abundance of flowers, but also because of the generosity of their foliage. The Persian silk tree (*Albizia julibrissin*), still a youngster in this picture, is now a large tree, but the dahlias and blue asters are still just as valuable for the colour they bring to the last fine autumn days at Giverny.

Monet adored sunflowers and painted them often, even before he came to live at Giverny. They are still planted here every year, for their spectacular flowers, of course, and also for their great height, which totally transforms the narrow flowerbeds. In September, they seem to reach up to the first floor windows, from which the painter would, no doubt, have admired them each morning.

Exhausted by their long flowering season, the roses willingly hand over
to the Virginia creeper (*Parthenocissus quinquefolia*) which now takes on its
magnificent glowing russet tones, with Boston ivy (*P. tricuspidata* 'Veitchii')
soon to follow. The red shades are repeated by the geraniums (*Pelargonium
zonale*) that are now filling the oval border just in front of the entrance steps.

DOUBLE-PAGE OVERLEAF
Perennial sunflowers (*Helianthus
decapetalus*) colonise the left-hand
flowerbed and mirror the annual
sunflowers in the bed on the right. This
abundance of yellow brings a sunshine
to the garden that can otherwise be
lacking at this time of year.

→ THE WATER GARDEN
THROUGH THE SEASONS

In 1893, Monet bought the meadow opposite
the *Clos Normand* with the intention of making
a water garden there. He diverted a branch of
the River Epte to fill the ponds that had been
dug at the end of the year. He laid out this
garden in a more naturalistic style, with exotic
trees and shrubs, then newly introduced to
Europe. There he had a bridge built in the
Japanese style, against which he planted two
different wisterias, in order to get a longer
flowering season. Even though the bridge has
been changed, the wisterias are still the same
ones. They vie with the waterlilies of every
colour that throng the pond throughout
summer. The water garden also owes much
of its beauty to the reflections of the sky
and of the plants floating on the water's surface,
reflections that captivated and inspired the
painter every day of his life at Giverny.

RIGHT
The large paulownia (*Paulownia
tomentosa,* syn. *P. imperialis*) makes a
link between the two parts of the garden.
In the *Clos,* it echoes the mauve of the
irises, and here, in the water garden, its
reflection brightens the surface of the pool
before the first waterlily flowers open.

In April, it is the shrubs clothing the banks of the pond that are this garden's stars. Brilliant red Japanese azaleas blaze among the Japanese maples (*Acer palmatum*), with their foliage of red (left) or fresh green (right). A flowering crab apple (*Malus floribunda*) illuminates the planting against the boundary wall running alongside the road that separates the two parts of the garden.

From the first fine days of spring, the young leaves of the weeping willow
enliven its cascade of yellow branches that partly mask the Japanese bridge.
The famous wisterias are still dormant and the waterlilies have barely
emerged, but the beauty of the reflection gives an extra dimension of
interest to this tranquil scene. It is the main focus of this garden.

In the grove of trees close to the bamboos, the spectacular pink blossom
of a Judas tree (*Cercis siliquastrum*) prolongs the great show put on by the
Japanese cherries. This small tree produces flowers straight from its trunk
and branches. In summer, its almost circular leaves make a pretty contrast
with the bamboo foliage in the background.

All through the winter, even without any leaves, the wisteria is still interesting.
Its long, twining branches with their many twists and turns are fascinating,
as is the way in which they hug the handrails and uprights of the bridge.
In just a few days these sinuous coils will disappear beneath, first,
the wisteria's flowers, then its abundant foliage.

In late April or early May (depending on the year), the Chinese wisteria (*Wisteria sinensis*) produces its short, but numerous, clusters of flowers on its still-bare branches. Planted just to its left, a lilac (*Syringa vulgaris*) provides a perfect harmony for several days.

LEFT
At the end of April and the beginning of May, tulip 'Shirley' brings some splashes of colour to harmonise with the carpet of forget-me-nots and the last fragrant narcissus flowers on the bank, overhung by a purple smoke-bush (*Cotinus coggygria* 'Royal Purple').

DOUBLE-PAGE OVERLEAF
The view from the bridge, framed by wisteria blossom, looking towards the fresh green weeping willows and purple cotinus.

The white Japanese wisteria (*Wisteria floribunda* 'Alba') takes over the reins, starting to flower around mid-May. More strongly scented than its Chinese cousin, its longer racemes of flower are produced with its fresh green leaves.

LEFT
The Chinese wisteria (*Wisteria sinensis*) planted on the side nearest the *Clos Normand* is first to flower, before producing its leaves.

As in the garden of the *Clos*, tulips and wallflowers bloom together, colouring the banks, while waiting for the herbaceous perennials to get into their stride. This beautiful black cultivar (*Tulipa* 'Queen of Night') stays in flower for a long period and makes a perfect contrast with orange Siberian wallflowers (*Erysimum* x *marshallii*, syn. *Cheiranthus allionii*) and forget-me-nots (*Myosotis biennis*).

RIGHT
At the end of May the foliage becomes denser, filtering the rays of the setting sun, making the reflections seem ever deeper. The rafts of waterlily leaves enlarge while the Siberian irises (*Iris sibirica*) come into flower on the banks.

The beginning of summer is marked by the opening of the waterlilies. Monet
would have been one of the first people to grow the coloured-flowered hybrids,
mostly bred by Latour Marliac in the Lot region, in south west of France.

LEFT
A magnificent harmony between the waterlilies and a great wave of astilbes
(*Astilbe* x *arendsii*) of the same soft pink. The boundary between earth and
water becomes ever more fluid.

In August, mophead hydrangeas flower along the banks, their colours repeating the pinks or reds of the waterlilies. When the astilbes have faded, their seedheads are left standing because they take on pretty tints of fawn and mahogany in autumn and early winter.

Even without flowers, the pond is still attractive. The linear contrasts
of the leaves, whether narrow and dangling, upright and sword-like,
horizontal and luxuriant, or in rounded masses, make up a picture
that will never lose its allure.

LEFT
Weeping willow and waterlilies, a source of infinite inspiration
for the painter – and, today, for photographers.

In November, the interplay of colours gradually blurs and softens, although
some autumn colour still sporadically lights up the banks of the pond.
The waterlily leaves dissolve and disappear little by little.
The garden begins to fall asleep...

LEFT
Once the play of colours and textures is over, only the different shapes
of the trees – weeping, upright, spreading or bushy – will remain to
delight the eyes of the gardeners, the only people who are
privileged to enjoy the garden during winter.

DOUBLE-PAGE OVERLEAF
Liquidambar styraciflua and swamp cypresses
(*Taxodium distichum*) bring colour to
the last days of autumn.

MONET'S GARDEN

OPENING TIMES
Every day, from 1 April to 31 October,
from 09.30 to 18.00

LOCATION
Close to Vernon, (70km west of Paris)
in the Department of l'Eure

ADDRESS
Fondation Claude Monet
84, rue Claude Monet
27620 Giverny

CONTACT
- email: contac@fondation-monet.com
- website: www.fondation-monet.com
- telephone: (in France) 02 32 51 28 21
              (from abroad) +33 2 32 51 28 21

The garden continues to inspire numerous painters, amateur and
professional. Monet's garden is open to them by prior arrangement.

PHOTOGRAPHIC CREDITS

All the photographs are by
Brigitte and Philippe Perdereau

except for:
Didier Willery, p5.

ISBN: 978-2-84138-465-5
2010 Les Editions Eugen Ulmer
8, rue Blanche 75009 Paris France
Tél.: 01 48 05 03 03 — Fax: 01 48 05 02 04
www.editions-ulmer.fr
Graphic design: Guillaume Duprat
Editor: Didier Willery
English translation: Simon Garbutt
Printing: Gruppo Editoriale Zanardi
Copyright registration : may 2010
Printed in Italy
N° edition : 465-01